MW00885990

This NoteBook Belongs to

home
SWEET
home

Stay Home
Stay Safe

Made in the USA
Monee, IL
07 October 2020

44241560R00057